Meldrum Academy

This book must be returned to the library on or before the date below

ABOUT TIME

Latitude & Longitude

Brian Williams

CHERRYTREE BOOKS

Published by CHERRYTREE PRESS
327 High Street
Slough
Berkshire
SL1 1TX

Created and designed by
THE FOUNDRY DESIGN AND PRODUCTION
Crabtree Hall, Crabtree Lane, Fulham, London, SW6 6TY

Special thanks to Lucy Bradbury, Vicky Garrard and the late Helen Courtney

British Library Cataloguing in Publication data.
Williams, Brian, 1943 Oct. 7-
Latitude and longitude. - (About time)
Juvenile literature 2.Longitude - Juvenile literature
I.Title
526.6'1
ISBN 182341278

First published 2002

Printed in Hong Kong by Wing King Tong Co. Ltd

Acknowledgements

The author and publishers would like to thank the following for permission to reproduce
Photographs: Front cover and Title page Science Museum/Science & Society Libraary and
Digital Vision Ltd page 4 Hereford Cathedral, Herefordshire/The Bridgeman Art Library page 5
(top) Bridgeman Art Library (bottom) Maximilian Stock Ltd/Science Photo Library page 6 (top)
Ancient Art and Architecture Collection Ltd/Bridgeman Art Library page 7 Mary Evans Picture
Library page 8 (top) Science Museum/Science & Society (bottom) Royal Geographical Society,
London/Bridgeman Art Library page 9 Universitatsbibliothek, Heidelberg,
Germany/Bridgeman Art Library page 10 (top) British Musem/Bridgeman Art Library (bottom)
Private Collection/Bridgeman Art Library p11 Christie's Images page 12 Science
Museum/Science & Society page 13 (top) Prado, Madrid, Spain/Bridgeman Art Library
(bottom) Royal Geographical Society, London/Bridgeman Art Library page 14 (top) Bridgeman
Giraudon/Lauros (bottom) Royal Geographical Society/Bridgeman Art Library page 16
(bottom) National Maritime Museum page 17 Private Collection/Bridgeman Art Library page
18 Science Museum/Science & Society page 19 Science Museum/Science & Society page 20
(top) Science Museum/Science & Society page 20 bottom, 21 and 22 (top) National Maritime
Museum page 22 (bottom) Topham Picturepoint page 23 Science Museum/Science & Society
page 24 (top) Topham Picturepoint (bottom) John Bethell/Bridgeman Art Library page 25
Science Museum/Science & Society page 26 Bridgeman Art Library page 28 Ton
Kingsbergen/Science Photo Library page 29 (top) David Parker/Science Photo Library (bottom)
GE Astro Space/Science Photo Library All graphics (6, 15, 16, 27) are courtesy of Foundry Arts.

Contents

Introduction

TIME AND TRAVEL

What time does the plane take off? How long will it take to drive to the airport? How long is the flight? How do pilots find their way, flying above the clouds? Every journey involves questions to do with time. If people could not measure time, they could not find the way across land, through the air, across the oceans or out into space. Nobody would ever arrive 'on time'.

FINDING THE WAY

In prehistoric times, a hunter could tell how long he had been away from home by noting the position of the Sun in the sky. The fact that the Sun rose every morning in the east and set every evening in the west, made it easier for early humans to find their way. At night, they learned to use the stars as guides.

The first maps were pictures of journeys. The first map-makers were people who, like the Ancient Egyptians, were good at maths and at keeping time. The Egyptians drew maps to show how much land each farmer had. Map-makers figured out how to show map-distances to scale, so a map could show which fields were bigger than others, or how far one town was from another.

The Mappa Mundi is displayed in Hereford Cathedral, England. A map of the world made in about 1290, it shows the Earth as a flat disk, with Europe, Africa and Asia surrounded by ocean.

PICTURING THE WORLD

Many early maps were hugely inaccurate, with large chunks of land missed out and blank spaces filled with pictures of the fantastic animals, giants and monsters a traveller might meet. As knowledge of the world increased, so maps improved.

Ancient people wondered what shape the world was. People in Peru thought it was square while Hindus in India believed the world was a half-globe, resting on the backs of four elephants which stood on the curved shell of a giant turtle while floating in the ocean. Greek scientists at first believed the Earth was flat, but eventually they decided it must be round, because that made better mathematical sense.

The Greeks also divided the Earth into two zones, north and south of the equator (the Earth's 'middle'), which were based on the different lengths of the days observed by travellers. The Chinese did the same, and soon map-makers were creating maps with lines which ran from north to south as well as from east to west, making a grid pattern. Using this grid, a traveller would be able to locate any place on Earth. It seemed so simple.

This picture from the 1300s shows Europeans all at sea. With only a compass and the stars to guide them, finding the way was a problem for seamen who strayed out of sight of familiar land.

ALL AT SEA

A map, however, is not much use if you have no idea how far you have gone. Before the thirteenth century, the only clocks were water-clocks, sundials and candle-clocks, none of which were much help to a sailor at sea. Even with better maps, sailors still got lost.

This book looks at how the clock came to the rescue of the sailors at sea, and how navigation became a science. Solving what scientists in the eighteenth century called 'the longitude problem' made possible the world of today, a world in which airliners criss-cross the continents and space probes home in on distant planets. Time turned out to be the key to finding the way – and returning safely.

Modern sailors can learn navigation on land, using a virtual reality simulator. This is the view a trainee tanker skipper gets, with the radar screen (right) scanning the busy sea lanes.

Knowing the Way

HOW BIG IS THE WORLD?

People in Ancient Greece knew the world was round. A scientist named Eratosthenes wanted to measure the distance around it. Eratosthenes was born in North Africa around 276 BC. He was so clever he was put in charge of the great library of Alexandria in Egypt. Stars, calendars and the shape of the world all fascinated him. One day he heard a curious story about a well at Syene (modern Aswan), to the south of Alexandria. On midsummer day at noon, the Sun's reflection could be seen in the water at the bottom. This must mean that the Sun was directly overhead as it cast no shadow. Eratosthenes knew that at the same time in Alexandria the Sun did cast a shadow. This gave him an idea of how to measure the Earth.

Eratosthenes was born in North Africa in about 276 BC. As well as calculating the Earth's circumference, he worked out how far the planet tilts on its axis and drew up a calendar of world events beginning from the Trojan War.

ERATOSTHENES TOTS IT UP

First, Eratosthenes measured the shadow cast by a pillar near his home. Then, using geometry, he worked out how far the Sun was from being directly overhead. It was about seven degrees, or roughly one-fiftieth of a circle, which has 360 degrees. From Aswan to Alexandria must therefore be one-fiftieth of the distance around the Earth.

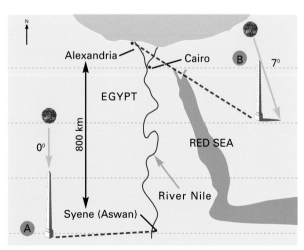

Eratosthenes asked travellers how long it took to journey between the two places. They said 50 days by camel. How fast does a camel walk? About 100 Greek *stadia* (roughly 20 km) a day. He then worked out the distance: 50 x 100 stadia = 5,000 stadia (some 800 km). When he multiplied this by 50 to get the earth's full circle he got a figure equal to 40,000 km. The actual distance is 40,075 km so he was remarkably accurate.

At Syene (A) the Sun was directly overhead at noon, while at Alexandria (B) it cast a shadow, the angle of which Eratosthenes measured. Using this figure he calculated that the Earth was round. He then calculated the distance around the Earth.

GREEKS AND GRIDS

Eratosthenes was a fine mathematician. In his day, scientists were better at measuring angles than at measuring distances. Maps were very sketchy because they were based on travellers' tales that were often wildly exaggerated. The best maps showed roads, oases, rivers and towns, but were vague about how far one place was from another.

The greatest Greek astronomer was Hipparchus (born around 190 BC). He was the first scientist to try fixing a place's position on Earth by its latitude and longitude. He worked out latitude by comparing the lengths of the shortest and longest days at the same place, and suggested using eclipses of the Sun, viewed from different places, for finding longitude. Hipparchus divided the world into zones according to their climates. He made a list of all the stars, and he worked out how long a year was to within 6.5 minutes.

By this time Greek maps were now more accurate, with parallel lines on them which made a grid. These lines are called 'meridians'. Some were drawn north–south (like lines of longitude) between famous places. Other lines were drawn east–west, parallel to the equator (like lines of latitude) to show the climate zones.

Greek scientists, like Hipparchus who is shown here, had no telescopes. Viewing tubes helped them concentrate on a particular star.

KEY DATES

▶ *c.*260 BC Eratosthenes works out the circumference of the Earth
▶ *c.*140 BC Hipparchus has a go at fixing latitude and longitude
▶ *c.*AD 150 Ptolemy is at work in Egypt; his book *Geography* includes a map of the world and list of places, with grid references – an early use of latitude and longitude (see page 8)
▶ AD 900 Chinese maps show the Chinese empire, on a grid and to scale, with north at the top

PTOLEMY GETS IT WRONG

Ptolemy, a Greek living in Egypt in the second century AD, made the most famous maps in the ancient world. People copied them for the next 1,500 years – and so repeated Ptolemy's huge mistake. He had marked his map in degrees, but he made each degree too small – roughly 80 km across, instead of 112 km. This error made places appear closer together and oceans look smaller than they really were. Sailors relying on Ptolemy's maps, as Christopher Columbus did when he set off on his famous journey in 1492, were in for some nasty surprises!

This illustration of 1535 shows Ptolemy, 'king' of ancient geographers and astronomers. His maps and geography books, including their errors, were copied and studied for 1,500 years

A SQUARE WORLD

Unlike the Greeks, the Ancient Chinese thought the world was flat. Despite this, they made excellent maps. The emperor of China in the third century AD could inspect a huge map of his empire drawn on a grid of criss-cross lines, like a chess board. The lines helped fix a particular point, and by the AD 900s north was always shown at the top, as it is today.

Chinese maps were drawn to scale: 2.5 cm on the map represented 100 li (roughly 54 km), so distances between places could be shown with some accuracy.

This map of the world was published in Germany in 1482 and was based on Ptolemy's ancient map. It shows only three continents (Europe, Africa and Asia) and the Indian Ocean.

SEARCHING FOR PARADISE

Some Christian voyagers hoped they might land in the Garden of Eden, the Paradise from which Adam and Eve had been expelled according to the Bible story. In the early AD 500s, an Irish monk named Brendan sailed a tiny leather boat west across the Atlantic Ocean. He came back with tales of an island he called 'The Promised Land' – which may have been America. Brendan's mysterious island was shown on maps for 1,000 years before explorers lost hope of finding the Garden of Eden.

▽ *The voyage and adventures of the Irish monk, Brendan, inspired many books. This picture, from a German book (c.1476), shows the intrepid monk in his boat meeting a fiery-looking New World inhabitant.*

GOING TO SEA

The first maps showed only the land in any detail, including a few places, rivers and perhaps the names of local tribes. The sea was left blank, except where islands were known to lie close to land. Sailors kept land in sight whenever they could, following the shore or 'hopping' from island to island.

When they ventured out of sight of land, sailors learned to find their way using the Sun (which always set in the west), by observing certain stars (such as the Pole Star) and by watching which way birds flew or currents flowed. With the stars to guide them, Polynesians sailed across the Pacific as far south as Australia, and Vikings from Scandinavia crossed the Atlantic to North America.

Early Exploration

EXPLORING THE MEDITERRANEAN

More than 3,000 years ago, Egyptians, Phoenicians and Greeks explored the Mediterranean Sea by sailing between the islands and along the coast. They noted landmarks such as mountain peaks, bays and dangerous rocks. Sometimes they wrote guides which could then be used by other sailors. Few sailors in those days could read, however, and a wise sailor listened to advice from others who had gone in the same direction – and returned. The best maps were the memories of experienced seamen.

The Phoenicians explored as far north as Britain and as far south as Africa in oared ships like this one from a stone carving dating from around 600 BC.

WITHOUT MAPS ACROSS OCEANS

The Vikings sailed from Denmark and Norway in the ninth century AD, their narrow longships crammed with swords, axes, food, and often wives, children and farm animals. They had no charts and so they relied on advice from sailors who had gone before them – such as 'steer south of Iceland so that you can sight birds and whales'. They knew the direction of the 'four winds' (North, South, East, West), but although they may have known about the strange behaviour of 'lodestones' (natural magnets), they had no compasses. Despite this, they were able to cross the Atlantic Ocean.

Long voyages were made in the Pacific, too. Voyagers in canoes took sticks and shells with them; these were arranged in patterns to show sailing directions from one island to the next.

 Viking ships had a single square sail and up to 60 oars. The ship was steered by a big steering oar, fixed on the right or 'steer-board' side, from which comes the term 'starboard'.

AT LAST, A MAP

It was not until the fourteenth century that the first proper sea-maps appeared. The Crusades brought map-makers extra business, as ships filled with soldiers and treasure-hunters lumbered slowly to and from the Holy Land. Mediterranean sailors began using charts on which lines were drawn to show the safe routes in and out of ports. These *portolanos* (Italian for 'harbour guides') were more accurate than land-maps, which were full of mistakes and scary pictures showing the presence of giants, dragons and sea serpents.

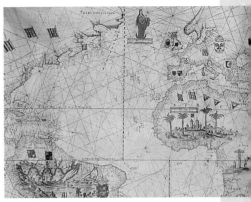

A sixteenth-century sailors' map of the Atlantic Ocean. The radiating lines on this portolano chart, similar to the lines on the compass, helped sailors set a course from one port to another.

INTO THE OPEN OCEAN

The world's oceans remained blank spaces on maps until the 1400s. At this time the Turks began to prevent Westerners from using the famous Silk Road, a network of overland trade routes between Europe and Asia. This was a disaster for European traders – they had to find a new route. To reach India, China and the spice islands of Indonesia, Europeans had to explore seas that they had never sailed in before.

The Portuguese made the first bold moves. They sent ships west into the Atlantic and south along the coast of Africa. The Mediterranean is a narrow sea, in which sailors seldom got lost for long. The Atlantic was quite different, though. As the Portuguese sailed out into this unknown ocean, they discovered not only how big it was, but also how terrifying its storms could be. Finding the way across this ocean was a fight for survival.

KEY DATES

▶ **AD 986** Vikings first sight North America, and land there in 1001

▶ **1100s** The magnetic compass is first used in Europe

▶ **1150** The Arab geographer Al-Idrisi makes a world map, using a grid; Arab traders had probably seen Chinese grid-maps

▶ *c.***1300s** *Portolanos* or harbour guides are used by Mediterranean sailors

▶ **1340s** The cross-staff is used by European sailors to take sightings of the Sun or a star

▶ **1375** The Great Catalan Atlas, drawn by Abraham Cresques in Spain, shows the Mediterranean coasts, part of Asia and the edge of the 'Western Ocean' (the Atlantic)

▶ **1430s** A European map shows 'Vinland', the long-abandoned Viking settlement in North America; the Portuguese set sail on the Atlantic; Prince Henry the Navigator sets up a school of navigation

▶ **1492** Christopher Columbus sails from Spain to the West Indies (see pages 12 and 13)

Navigation Aids

To help them, the explorers now had some navigation aids. Most importantly, they could find north using a magnetic compass. The compass was a Chinese invention that finally made its way to the West in the thirteenth century. With simple tools such as a wooden cross-staff, seafarers measured the angle of the Sun above the horizon so that they could fix their latitude – how far north or south of the equator their ship was.

To find how fast the ship was going, a sailor threw a long, knotted rope into the water and counted the knots as the rope ran through his fingers. Checking the time with a sand-glass, he could then work out the ship's speed in 'knots' an hour. In this way, using 'dead' (deduced or 'worked out') reckoning, a sailor could tell how far the ship had travelled in a day.

In shallow waters, sailors checked the depth by lowering a 'lead line', a rope with a lead weight on the end. An experienced seaman could tell where he was by the direction of the winds, the mud on the seabed, or the colour of the water.

Using a cross-staff, a seaman could measure the angle of the Sun or a star, to find the position of latitude. Different cross-pieces could be fitted to slide along the staff, which was marked with a scale.

NEW WORLD ADVENTURERS

With each new voyage, the Portuguese were able to add new details to their maps. Their commander, Prince Henry 'the Navigator', made map-making as important as shipbuilding.

By 1488, Portuguese ships had sailed south to South Africa's Cape of Good Hope. Within the next 10 years they had reached India. Their ships were guided across the Arabian Sea by an Arab pilot named Ibn Majid, who had written the best navigation book in the Arabic language.

COLUMBUS GETS IT WRONG

Ibn Majid's maps of the Indian Ocean – a sea well known to Arab, Indian and Chinese sailors – were better than any maps of the Atlantic. In Spain, trying to raise funds for a voyage west across the Atlantic, Christopher Columbus pointed to the ancient (but inaccurate) maps of Ptolemy as proof that the ocean was not very wide. He was sure that Asia was only a few days' sailing away.

When he set off in 1492, how surprised Columbus was when the voyage lasted three weeks! He and his men were even more surprised to discover a New World, instead of Asia as they had planned. The mysterious 'Wineland' or Vinland of Viking tales turned out to be real. Another continent, America, was added to the map.

Columbus and his men land in the New World, truly thankful to set foot on dry land again after three weeks at sea. They eventually realised they were not in Asia as expected.

THE MAGIC NEEDLE

The first compasses were very simple – a magnetised iron needle floating on a piece of cork, so it could turn freely to show north. Alongside was a card marked with north, south, east and west. The card was turned to line up with the direction of the needle. By the 1300s, better compasses had the card floating too, so that it turned with the needle. It was like magic, and a ship's captain kept his 'magic' compass in a closed box, for secrecy.

The compass in this form was devised in China, and in use by European sailors by the sixteenth century. The card shows the four 'cardinal' points (N, S, E, W), as well as NE, SE, SW, NW and the 360 degrees of a circle.

13

Maps and Mysteries

LUCKY WITHOUT LONGITUDE

Christopher Columbus was lucky that he did not get dangerously lost. So were the first round-the-world voyagers (or 'circumnavigators') Juan Sebastian del Cano and Francis Drake. Although experienced seamen, they might easily have vanished from history as many ships did. No sailor could be sure he wasn't 'all at sea', because he could not keep time accurately, and so could not pinpoint where he was on the map.

MAP PROJECTIONS

By the late 1500s, better maps had begun to appear in Europe. There were even round globes. Map-makers had worked out how to draw a globe-shaped area (the Earth) on a flat sheet of paper. The shapes of land and sea have to be stretched or shrunk, and to do this map-makers use a kind of mathematics called a 'map projection'.

The first map-making system accurate enough to be useful to sailors was made in 1569. It is still called the Mercator projection, after the Flemish (Belgian) map-maker, named Gerardus Mercator, who invented it. On a Mercator map, directions between two points are always straight lines. This is useful, but to get it right, a Mercator map has to show landmasses at the wrong size. Greenland, for example, looks bigger than South America, when it is actually much smaller.

This globe from Germany was made in 1492 – the year Columbus sailed. The area of sea showing is the Indian Ocean.

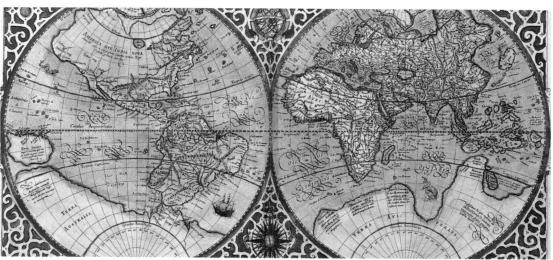

 In 1585 Mercator produced the first map-book to be called an 'atlas'. It contained this world map, probably the best of its day.

LATITUDE...

Latitude lines are the east–west lines on a map. To find which latitude (north or south of the equator) his ship is in, a sailor can look for objects in the sky above the horizon – the Sun, Moon and stars such as the Pole Star.

Latitude is measured in degrees (°). Ptolemy made the equator the 0 degree line – the 'start and end' of latitude. The equator marks the point at which the Sun appears almost directly overhead. It divides the two 'halves' of the Earth, the northern and southern hemispheres.

At the 'top' of the map, the North Pole has a latitude of 90 degrees north; the South Pole has a latitude of 90 degrees south.

The equator is the imaginary line around the Earth's middle. Lines of latitude (in red) are shown encircling the globe, from 0 degrees at the equator to 90 degrees at the poles.

KEY DATES

▶ **1492**   Martin Behaim of Germany makes a globe of the world; it does not show America

▶ **1498**   Confirming that a sea route lay to the East, the Portuguese explorer Vasco da Gama sails around Africa's Cape of Good Hope and reaches India

▶ **1500s**   The first European maps show latitudes

▶ **1514**   The German astronomer Johannes Werner suggests a way of using the Moon and stars to work out longitude

▶ **1519–22**   The first voyage around the world is made by an expedition led by Ferdinand Magellan, a Porteguese sailing for Spain. Magellan was in fact killed in the East Indies after having crossed the Pacific, but one of the expedition's five ships completed the journey, commanded by Juan Sebastian del Cano, a Spanish captain.

▶ **1569**   The Flemish map-maker Gerardus Mercator produces the first map drawn on a new projection that makes a path in any direction appear as a straight line

▶ **1579–80**   Francis Drake of England completes the second circumnavigation of the Earth

... AND LONGITUDE

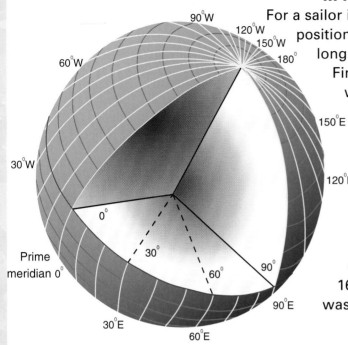

For a sailor in the 1600s, finding latitude (the position north or south) was fairly simple as long as he could see the Sun or the stars. Finding longitude (the position east or west) was not so easy, no matter how clear the skies.

On a map, the lines of longitude run north–south. By counting off degrees of longitude as the lines are crossed, a traveller can find out how far east or west he has travelled. Today, the 'starting point' is the Greenwich Meridian, the line of 0 degrees longitude. But in the 1600s there was no such line. Nothing was fixed.

Lines of longitude (in yellow) encircle the globe east and west of the 'prime meridian' or line of 0 degrees longitude. Knowing both latitude and longitude, a traveller can fix a position precisely.

NAVIGATING BY CLOCKS

A sailor could not peer at the Sun or stars to fix his longitude. He needed two clocks: one to show the time on his ship (checked at noon against the Sun), the other to show the exact time back at his home port, or some other point at a known position. By comparing the times, he could work out how far his ship had sailed.

If a navigator could know his ship's latitude and longitude, he could plot a course and fix his position exactly. All he had to do was mark where lines crossed on the map. This is called a co-ordinate.

By measuring the angle of stars above the horizon an astrolabe found latitude. A sailor could then work out the time. This night astrolabe, or nocturnal, is from 1589.

THE CLOCK'S WRONG

Some maths – and two clocks – could therefore help to prevent sailors getting lost. However, even the best clocks of the seventeenth century were pretty unreliable: even if they were quietly ticking away indoors, no two clocks kept the same time for long. They began to run fast or slow, or stopped altogether and had to be wound up again. Certainly no clock could be trusted on a ship that was tossed by waves, boiled by the tropical Sun or frozen by Arctic ice. Without a new, super-reliable clock, sailors would remain all at sea.

WHERE ARE YOU? FIND OUT IN A COUPLE OF TICKS

The Earth turns round through 360 degrees every 24 hours. Divide 360 by 24, and you get 15 degrees – the distance the Earth turns in an hour. The Earth is widest at the equator, where a degree is about 112 km across. Let's say you were in a ship at the equator sailing west. You have two clocks: one shows the time on the ship (set each day by the Sun at noon); the other clock shows the time in the port you left several days ago. The times will not be the same. If there is an hour's difference, the ship has sailed fifteen degrees. That's 15 x 112 km: answer 1,680 km.

This map of 1559 shows the Pacific Ocean and part of South America, with the equator (just south of Quito). It clearly shows lines of latitude and longitude (the point at which they meet is called a co-ordinate). The ship is Ferdinand Magellan's.

17

The Pendulum Swings

GALILEO GETS RHYTHM

Clocks were getting better. In 1582 the Italian scientist Galileo had noticed that a lamp on a chain swung in a perfectly regular rhythm. This chance observation led to the invention of the pendulum, and later the pendulum clock. The pendulum made the clock a much better time-keeper. Where previous clocks had only hour hands, clocks in the seventeenth century had minute and second hands. By 1700, the regular tick-tock of the clock was a familiar sound in houses and workplaces.

But a pendulum needed to be kept level, so it would be no use at sea. It also behaved oddly when too hot or too cold because the metal it was made of expanded or contracted. The longitude problem remained.

A model of a pendulum clock designed by Galileo shortly before he died. He realised that a swinging pendulum could control a clock, whether the clock was driven by weights or springs.

THE SUMS IN THE STARS

Perhaps the answer was in the stars. In new observatories built in Britain and France, astronomers clustered around telescopes. They peered at the Moon. They scanned the distant planet Jupiter to see if the regular eclipses of its moons might make 'universal timekeepers'. They drew up star-maps, charts and tables of figures showing the movements of the planets and their moons.

All this was useful information, but the sums needed to work out longitude from star-charts challenged the astronomer at his desk. They were a nightmare for ships' officers and crews – even those who now studied maths as part of their navigation training.

DISASTER AT SEA

Most ship's navigators went on using the old methods. They took sightings of the Sun, Moon and stars, and checked them against tables (lists of numbers) that gave star positions through the year. A tiny mistake could result in a ship wandering dangerously off course. In 1707, disaster struck a squadron of British Navy ships close to home. Under the command of Admiral Sir Clowdisley Shovell, the ships got lost heading into the English Channel and strayed too near the Scilly Isles. Believing they were safe in clear water, the sailors were horrified to see rocks looming out of the mist. Four ships, including the admiral's ship *Association,* sank and 2,000 men drowned.

This awful loss, so near home, was a national scandal. Something had to be done. In 1714, the British government offered a prize of £20,000 (over £6 million in today's money) to anyone who could solve the longitude problem. To win the prize, the inventor must make a clock so reliable that it would not lose or gain more than three seconds in a day. It must be able to cross the Atlantic – a 40-day voyage – and find longitude within half a degree (two minutes of time).

A MAGIC CLOCK

Many scientists doubted that such a clock could ever be made. In the meantime people began considering what else might work. Suggestions included firing cannon into the sky at regular intervals, so ships could spot the exploding shells but most sensible experts agreed that the only answer was a magic clock, a clock that would work at sea and in all weathers.

Many astronomers, including Galileo Galilei (1564-1642), tried to solve the longitude problem by star-gazing. Galileo thought the moons of Jupiter would be a reliable 'clock', but the pendulum was more practical, at least on dry land.

KEY DATES

▶ **1582**   Galileo discovers the principle of the pendulum
▶ **1596**   John Davis invents the back-staff, easier to use than the cross-staff because the observer had the Sun at his back and so was not dazzled
▶ **1610**   Galileo observes the sky through a telescope; he suggests the moons of the planet Jupiter could be used to help sailors solve the longitude problem
▶ **1637**   Galileo suggests that a pendulum clock might be a better solution
▶ **1657**   Christiaan Huygens demonstrates his new pendulum clock, but trials of pendulums on ships prove that they don't work well in rough seas
▶ **1668**   Italian astronomer Giovanni Cassini publishes a set of tables for finding longitude, based on the moons of Jupiter
▶ **1675**   The new Royal Observatory at Greenwich, England, is one of several new centres for star-gazing

The Time Has Come

ENTER MR HARRISON

The man who surprised all the experts walked into London from the north of England. His name was John Harrison. Harrison was born in 1693 at Foulby, a village near Hull in Yorkshire. A carpenter's son, he taught himself clockmaking simply because he was interested in it, and he made his first clock in 1713.

John Harrison was good at finding answers to problems. He tried making clock parts from naturally oily wood, not iron or steel, and found that the clockwork did not need oiling and did not rust. He invented a pendulum made of strips of brass and steel which worked better because it swung at the same rate no matter whether the day was hot or cold. He made a new escapement – the ticking mechanism that regulates the clock – known as the 'grasshopper' because it had long legs. He set his clocks by the stars, as he watched them move in the sky against the outline of the chimney and window-frame of his house.

Harrison heard of the prize offered by the Board of Longitude. In 1730 he travelled south to London, to the Greenwich Observatory, where he met Edmond Halley, the Astronomer Royal. He swapped ideas with a London clockmaker called George Graham. Then he went home to begin work on a clock that would keep accurate time at sea.

▲ *John Harrison spent his life making clocks; he was determined to crack the longitude problem and win the prize offered by the British government.*

THE FIRST H-CLOCKS

For five years Harrison worked on his first sea-clock or 'chronometer'. Clock experts call it H-1 as it was Harrison's first design. In 1735, H-1 was ready and Harrison took it to sea on a trial voyage to Lisbon in Portugal. The new clock had no pendulum; it was kept to time by balances and springs. It lost less than 10 seconds a day, but Harrison knew he could do better. He set to work on a second clock, to win the prize.

▶ *Harrison's H-1 took five years to make. It had four dials, showing hours, minutes, seconds and days of the month, and weighed 34 kg.*

H-2 AND H-3

Another six years went by before H-2 was ready in 1741. Although it passed all its trials on land, running smoothly even when heated, cooled and shaken, Harrison was still not satisfied. H-2 was never tested at sea.

Back into the workshop he went. Years passed before, in 1759, he completed a third clock. H-3 had more than 750 parts, all made by John Harrison and his son, William. Regulated by an intricate arrangement of balanced weights, springs and metal ribbons, H-3 was smaller and lighter than either H-1 or H-2. But still Harrison felt it wasn't right; it was still too big.

 *Harrison's H-3 was the first clock designed to be unaffected by changes in temperature, and had ball bearings to ease friction. It weighed 27 kg.*

KEY DATES

▶ **1707** The British warship *Association* and three others are wrecked after a navigation error

▶ **1714** The British government offers a prize for an answer to the longitude problem

▶ **1725** John Flamsteed's star catalogue is the first based on observation through a telescope

▶ **1731** Invention of the mirror sextant, by John Hadley in England and Thomas Godfrey in America; used at sea for measuring the angle between the Sun or a star and the horizon, it was better than older sighting instruments

▶ **1735** Harrison completes his first clock, H-1

Small is Beautiful

Some years before, Harrison had been given a pocket watch, made by a London clockmaker to his own orders. He took it to pieces and looked at it closely. The next day, he pushed aside his large clocks and set about making a new and much smaller clock (based on his pocket watch). Known as H-4, it was a miniature marvel of precision engineering. He was proud of it; this was the one to win the prize.

The H-3 and H-4 clocks were handed over for trials by the navy, but there were months of delay before the ship finally set sail in 1762. Harrison left H-3 behind, sending only H-4 to sea. Harrison's son, William, went with it, winding the watch every 30 hours during the voyage to Jamaica.

H-4 triumphed under the strictest tests. After 81 days at sea it had lost only five minutes – equivalent to 1.25 degrees of longitude. The longitude problem was solved.

H-4 was only 13 cm across, and weighed just 1.4 kg. Unlike the earlier H-clocks, its works needed oiling. To stop it wearing out, H-4 is not still ticking, unlike H-1.

CLOCKS GO TO SEA

The government now said H-4 was too valuable to be allowed to leave Britain. Harrison had to let his masterpiece be copied, for more tests. On his second voyage to the South Seas (1772–75), Captain James Cook took several sea-clocks. One was a copy of H-4 made by a clockmaker named Larcum Kendall. It was as reliable as the original, proving that Harrison's design was true. Cook wrote of the little watch as 'our trusty friend'.

Even after H-4's success, some astronomers still claimed the stars were more reliable than any clock. When John Harrison died in 1776, his fame was assured, but he had not been given the cash prize in full, nor the honours that his painstaking work had earned.

James Cook (1728-79) was a brilliant navigator. Trained in the old ways of seamanship, Cook knew that Harrison's new sea-clocks would save many lives.

A CLOCK FOR EVERY SAILOR

Other clockmakers such as Pierre Le Roy in France and Thomas Earnshaw in England also built chronometers. By the 1780s chronometers were being made cheaply enough for every naval officer to afford one. The ultimate in chronometers was probably the US Marine Chronometer of 1944, made by the Hamilton Watch Company, but the basic appearance of the 'sea-clock' changed little in 150 years.

WATCH AROUND THE WORLD

James Cook made three voyages of exploration between 1768 and 1779. When he first set sail from Britain, the Pacific Ocean was still largely unmapped. His first mission – as captain of a converted coal-ship named the *Endeavour* – was to visit the island of Tahiti and observe the planet Venus pass across the Sun. He went on to explore the coasts of New Zealand and land in Botany Bay in Australia, returning home in 1771.

In 1772 Cook was off again, this time in the *Resolution* and with the H-4 chronometer. He sailed south until he crossed the Antarctic Circle – the first explorer to do so. He crossed the Pacific, proving that there were no other unexplored southern continents apart from Australia and ice-covered Antarctica. In three years, he sailed 112,000 km, the longest voyage ever made.

Cook's last voyage began in 1776. *Resolution* returned to the Pacific, sailed to the islands of Hawaii, revisited New Zealand and then headed north as far as British Columbia and Alaska. His epic journey nearly over, Cook returned to Hawaii, where he was murdered by islanders.

Cook had proved that the longitude watch worked. A superb navigator, Cook was a captain who both cared for his crew and was painstaking in his science and map-making. His voyages filled in some of the last great blanks on the world map.

Now that longitude could be fixed with certainty, thanks to Harrison's clock, navigation was no longer a hit and miss adventure.

During his first voyage (1768-71) James Cook began to map Australia and New Zealand. Cook's ship, the Endeavour, is shown here beached and awaiting repairs in Australia.

Time and Travel

STEAM-SPEED

By the 1800s, sailors no longer feared getting lost. Stormy seas were always dangerous, but charts were more accurate and navigation had become a science. Steamships began to cross the oceans in the 1830s, and a steamship passenger set off at least knowing the day, if not the hour, when the ship would reach port.

The Industrial Revolution and new scientific discoveries were changing people's lives and the world seemed to be moving faster. The 1830s brought the first regular passenger steam trains, chugging along newly laid steel tracks between fast-growing towns and cities. Trains needed timetables to show when each trip began and ended. A train could not get lost but passengers often became confused, because clocks along the railway showed slightly different times!

Railways needed reliable timetables – useful for passengers and vital for train safety. The new telegraph (1837) was used to wire time signals along the track, to keep station clocks to time.

LOCAL TIME AND TROUBLE

People in one town kept one time; others to the east or west kept different times. Town clocks were set by the Sun as there were no radio or TV time checks. In Britain, Londoners set their clocks to 'Greenwich time', set by the Royal Observatory every day at noon. But noon in Bristol, a city west of London, was slightly later. So London time was not the same as Bristol time. This could cause problems.

In the 1850s British newspapers reported that a person facing a charge in the law court had lost his case because he arrived late. The court was due to start at 10 o'clock in the morning Greenwich time. But the defendant's clock was set to local Dorset time, which was nine minutes later. In the end, judges ruled that in such cases, 10 o'clock was when local people said it was.

The Royal Observatory at Greenwich set the time first for Britain and eventually for the world. The red ball drops every day at 1300 GMT (Greenwich Mean Time) as a time signal.

RAILWAY TIME

Timetabled trains had to have a standard time, so companies ran their trains by 'railway time'. They set all the station clocks along their track to the same time, and took no notice of local time. This made life very complicated: people using the trains had to make sure they knew which was which.

This muddle could not go on. By 1880, every clock in Britain was set to railway time, which was renamed Greenwich time. The United States of America had about 100 different 'railroad times', but in 1883 these were reduced to just four.

Telegraph machines for sending signals along a wire electrically were invented by Samuel Morse in the USA and by Charles Wheatstone and Fothergill Cooke (an example shown here) in Britain.

KEY DATES

▶ **1791** The Ordnance Survey, Britain's official mapping organisation, is founded

▶ **1840** Britain's Great Western Railway makes 'London Time' standard on all its stations

▶ **1852** Greenwich Observatory begins sending time signals by telegraph to post offices and public clocks

▶ **1879** United States Geological Survey, the US map-making organisation, is founded

▶ **1906** Guglielmo Marconi sends the first radio signals from ship to shore

▶ **1910** The first radio signals are sent from an aircraft to the ground

▶ **1933** The first air almanac shows the positions of stars for air navigators

▶ **1940s** Radar is developed to track aircraft and ships; radio beams are used to guide planes and rockets

▶ **1955** The first atomic clock

▶ **1964** The first navigation satellite in space

▶ **1995** The US Navstar Global Positioning System (GPS) satellite network starts working

The World goes Zonal

I n a huge country such as the United States, the time difference from east to west was hours, not minutes. There was a $3\frac{1}{2}$ hour difference in time between New York in the east and San Francisco in the west. A teacher named Charles Dowd suggested splitting the country into time zones, with the minute hand on clocks staying the same but the hour hand being moved one hour between one zone and the next.

THE GREENWICH MERIDIAN

Time zones could be set up around the world. But where would be the 'start line' for an international system of time zones? Every country thought it should have this start line.

Britain's Astronomer Royal, Sir George Biddell Airy, had been using a special telescope at Greenwich to observe the stars for navigation and timekeeping for years. Most ships sailing all over the world already used Greenwich as the meridian, or line of 0 degrees longitude, on their maps. Why not use this telescope as the marker for world time? In 1884, almost all the nations of the world met at Washington, D.C. in the United States and agreed that the Greenwich telescope should be the 'prime meridian'. France voted 'no', grumbling that Paris deserved the honour. France did not switch to Greenwich time until 1911.

The famous telescope is still at Greenwich, even though the Observatory's astronomers have now moved to clearer skies in the Canary Islands. Visitors to the old Greenwich Observatory can stand with their feet astride the meridian line marked on the ground outside. One foot is in the world's eastern hemisphere, the other in the western!

PRIME MERIDIAN
OF THE WORLD
EAST | WEST
LONGITUDE | LONGITUDE

Centre of Transit Circle
Latitude 51 28 38·2 north
Longitude 0 00 00'

The prime meridian at Greenwich marks the line of 0 degrees longitude, and passes through Flamsteed House, the original home of the Royal Observatory established by King Charles II in 1675.

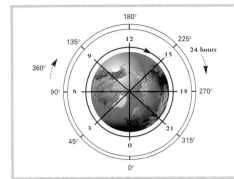

TIME AND DISTANCE

The Earth spins once every 24 hours, so:
24 hours = 360 degrees of longitude
1 hour = 15 degrees of longitude
4 minutes = 1 degree of longitude
1 minute = 15 seconds of longitude

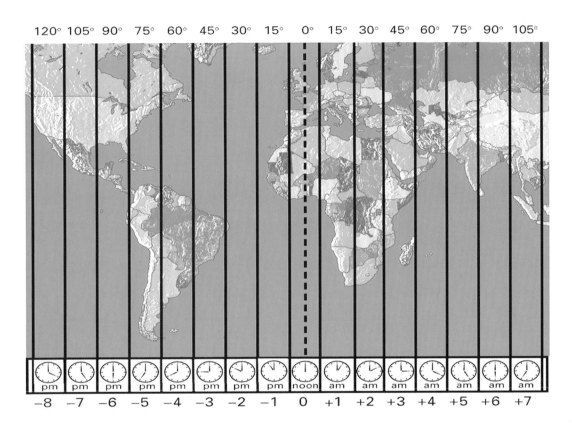

World time zones. Each 15-degree zone represents one hour. The clocks at the bottom indicate time difference, east (minus) and west (plus) of Greenwich. There are 24 zones in all, but only 16 are shown here.

WORLD TIME ZONES

There are 24 world time zones, 12 east of Greenwich and 12 west. The North and South Poles have their own time, with weeks of all-day sunlight and weeks of permanent night.

The United States and Canada have six time zones, with 15 degrees of longitude (and one hour of time) difference between each. The main zones, from east to west, are: Atlantic Time, Eastern Time, Central Time, Mountain Time, Pacific Time and Alaska Time. There are separate zones for Newfoundland in the east, and for the Hawaiian and Aleutian Islands in the west.

Timed to the Millionth

When the first quartz-crystal clocks were made in the 1930s, a new age of accurate timekeeping began. There was no more winding, no more moving clock hands to put the clock 'right'. The watch on your wrist keeps going for a year or so, and should keep perfect time as long as the battery lasts. Even more astonishingly, the atomic clocks used by scientists lose no more than seconds in millions of years!

Measurement, too, has become extraordinarily precise. In 1972 scientists used a laser to bounce a beam of light off a mirror placed on the Moon. By measuring how long the light took to travel back, they found the distance between the Earth and the Moon (356,000 km at its closest) to within 5 cm.

Map-makers no longer have to climb mountains and cross deserts, measuring as they go. Cameras in aircraft or in space satellites can scan vast areas of land and sea in a few hours. The pictures give detailed information from which all kinds of maps can be drawn.

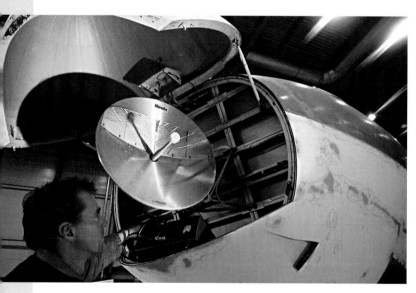

NAVIGATION TODAY

Do ships today get lost, like the sailing ships of old? Hardly ever. Nor do aircraft. What keeps supertankers and jumbo jets moving around the world, on course and on time? Navigation systems. Modern navigators rely on electronics – radio, radar and computers. These systems show sailors and pilots precisely where they are, at any time of day and night, and in all weathers.

Checking the radar in a civil airliner. All modern aircraft carry radar and navigational aids so precise that planes are kept at safe distances apart in crowded skies and can land automatically.

STILL STAR-GAZING

Some old rules still apply. To fix a position, any navigator must know how fast and far he or she has travelled, and so needs to measure time accurately. Ships and aircraft still use some methods familiar to Captain Cook, including dead reckoning and celestial (star) navigation. Navigators still observe the stars, checking against an almanac – a book of tables that show where each star-group is in the night sky at different times during the year.

SATELLITES IN SPACE

John Harrison (see page 20) was a star-gazer. Maybe he would have liked the idea of artificial stars as timekeepers. That's what satellites are – fixed stars, like guide-lights in the sky. The first satellites for navigation were launched into Earth orbit in the 1960s, and today's Navstar satellites provide a global network. Each satellite carries an atomic clock, so accurate it would have surprised even John Harrison. The satellites send out radio signals to show their position above the Earth and the precise time. The computer on a ship or plane picks up signals from three or more satellites, and from these 'fixes', it works out its own position.

Even a submarine's navigator can use the stars, observing them through a special star-gazing periscope. Underwater and moving 'blind', submarine crews rely on radar and sound-signals (sonar) to form pictures of the ocean around, and navigate using inertial guidance. In this system, computers constantly check the boat's movement against how far and how long it has travelled, working out its course and position as it glides through the ocean depths.

KNOWING WHERE WE ARE

So today almost everyone knows where they are. An explorer at the South Pole, a solo yacht sailor in the Pacific, a balloonist crossing the Alps, an astronaut in the Space Shuttle – they can all be linked by radio and computer so we can see on a map exactly where they are.

This would be unbelievable to any traveller of 100 years ago. To the brave seamen of the 1500s, it would seem like magic. One day, future voyagers may again go into the unknown – venturing into deep space, where there are no lines of latitude and longitude. Then once more the stars will be their guides.

 Using a hand-held satellite receiver any traveller can fix his or her position in seconds, using data from satellites orbiting the Earth. These devices are accurate to within 100 metres.

Glossary

Astronomer
A scientist who studies the stars and planets through observation.

Atlas
A book of maps.

Atomic Clocks
The most accurate clocks yet made; they count the electromagnetic waves given off or absorbed by atoms of caesium, hydrogen or ammonia.

Calendar
A chart or table showing the days, weeks and months of the year.

Chronometer
A sea-clock, an instrument for accurate measurement of time on ocean voyages.

Co-ordinate
The position on a map where lines of latitude and longitude, or other guidelines on a grid, cross.

Crusades
Religious wars between Christians and Muslims for control of the Holy Land (Palestine), between 1095 and 1270.

Day
The time from sunrise to sunset; it can also mean the 24-hour period from midnight to midnight.

Degree
A unit of measurement (temperature or the angle of a circle, for example). A circle has 360 degrees (shown as °).

Eclipse
The blocking of light from the Sun or the Moon. The Moon may pass between the Earth and the Sun (solar eclipse), or the Earth may block sunlight from reaching the Moon (lunar eclipse). Eclipses also happen on other planets.

Equator
An imaginary line around the widest point of the Earth, dividing the globe into two halves. The equator is the line of 0 degrees latitude.

Escapement
The device in a clock which regulates the movement of the pendulum or gear wheels by catching against a toothed wheel.

Explorer
A person who travels to previously little-known places to find out more about them.

Greenwich
A place in England beside the River Thames east of the City of London, now a London borough; it is the site of the Royal Greenwich Observatory and the prime meridian (0 degrees longitude).

Grid
Lines drawn parallel to one another at right angles, to form squares like those on a chess board.

Holy Land
Old name for Palestine, at the eastern end of the Mediterranean Sea, with holy places sacred to Jews, Christians and Muslims.

Latitude
The position of a point on the Earth's surface in relation to the equator; on a map, latitude is shown by lines running east to west.

Longitude
Lines on a map that run north to south.

Meridian
A line on a map showing longitude. Lines of latitude are sometimes called parallels.

Millennium
A period of 1,000 years, from the Latin *mille* (1,000) and *annus* (year).

Navigator
A person who directs the course of a ship, aeroplane or any other vehicle, following a map.

Observatory
A building where astronomers work and set up their telescopes.

Orbit
The path followed by a moon or planet as it moves around another body in space. The Moon orbits the Earth, and the Earth orbits the Sun.

Pendulum
A weighted metal rod that swings at a regular rate; in pendulum clocks, altering the position of the weight, or bob, makes the pendulum swing faster or slower – and so makes the clock run faster or slower.

Planet
A large body in space, orbiting a star.

Projection
A method of drawing to show a curved object (like the Earth) on a flat surface, such as a map.

Sand-glass
An early clock, in which sand trickled from one glass bulb into another very slowly, measuring time.

Satellite
A body circling another in space, such as a moon which circles a planet, or a spacecraft which circles the Earth.

Scale
On a map, a key showing what distance on the ground is represented by what distance on the map (for example, 1cm:1km means that one centimetre on the map represents one kilometre of actual distance).

Seasons
Part of the year; such as the four seasons of cool countries (spring, summer, autumn, winter).

Star
A huge ball of hot gas in space, giving off energy as light; the Sun is a medium-sized star.

Sun
The star around which the nine planets of our Solar System move in orbit.

Index